Lex Islamica: Islamic Law
for the New Millennium

Series Editors: Aamirah S. Nyazee & Ibrahim A. K. Nyazee

LEX ISLAMICA: ISLAMIC LAW FOR THE NEW MILLENNIUM

(Introduction to the Series)

Imran Ahsan Khan Nyazee

Advanced Legal Studies Institute
Islamabad

Advanced Legal Studies Institute,
Head Office: No. 103, Street 2, PTV Colony,
Shahpur, Islamabad,
Pakistan 44000

First Published: 2019

ADVANCED LEGAL STUDIES INSTITUTE

TABLE OF CONTENTS

PREFACE

The Lex Islamica Series is being launched to promote and develop Islamic law as international law. Islamic International Law so developed will be available for use by individual states as and when they need to benefit from it. For its development, Lex Islamica will employ *uṣūl al-fiqh* in a new form. To introduce this new form or methodology of *uṣūl*, two small books will be published with the following titles:

- The Original Meaning of Ḥanafī *Uṣūl al-Fiqh*: Sources and Discipline

- *Uṣūl al-Fiqh* for the New Millennium

The present book is a small introduction to the Series. This introduction visualizes modern Islamic law as the common law of all Muslims, a law that exists at the global level and is concerned with issues that may be found within individual states. For the details this book is to be read. It has intentionally been kept very concise and brief. A website will be created for the development of Lex Islamica. It will focus primarily on commercial law. If sufficient interest is shown by scholars and visitors, a journal may also be launched.

Imran Ahsan Khan Nyazee
Islamabad
December, 2017

CHAPTER 1

INTRODUCTION TO ISLAMIC LAW AS INTERNATIONAL LAW

فَقَالَ هٰؤُلَآءِ القَومِ لَا يَكَادُونَ يَفقَهونَ حَدِيثًا

What is wrong with these people that they fail to <u>understand</u> a simple statement (Qur'ān 4 : 78)

Islamic law is international law as it was laid down for all mankind. It began with this role and grew rapidly after its birth. Its growth slowed down as sultanates emerged at great distances; losing touch with the center. The rise of the Westphalian states finally arrested its growth in many areas. The reason for this was the monopolization of all law by the new creature called the "modern state."

Rapid changes in the world, in the last few decades, have now created an opportunity for Islamic law to rise again. This rise of Islamic law for the new millennium will not be through the coercive power of a modern state or even through physical domination. Its rise will come about through the rise of the Muslim Ummah meeting, participating and collaborating through cyberspace for the benefit and service of all humanity. This small book outlines and explains this dynamic framework that heralds the revival and development of this law with the help of a new methodology that has been left as a heritage by the ancestors.

Islamic law has a few distinctive features. We may list and discuss these briefly as this will facilitate the understanding of what is to follow.

The first feature is that Islamic law has been developed by private persons and not by rulers or governments. From the earliest times, the people organised themselves into schools of law and developed the law by interpreting the texts of the Qur'ān and the Sunnah for their needs. Guidance was sought in this process from the decisions of the Companions of the Prophet (pbuh). Matters of public law too—for example, criminal law and public revenue—were initially determined by the schools, and the rulers followed what these schools had laid down.

In its dramatic emergence on the world scene, Islamic law did not hesitate to borrow good things from the existing or earlier civilizations, especially the Greek and the Roman, whose works they translated in a systematic and enthusiastic manner. What they took from these civilization, however, was always first passed through a sieve created by the sources, general principles, and stringent methodology of Islamic law. Thus, the material borrowed was first "Islamized."

Most of the law worked on the basis of choices exercised by the people. The first choice in this context meant the choosing of a school. Choosing a school meant choosing an internally consistent package. There was complete freedom in the exercise of such choices, and all choices were given full respect. There was no compulsion in the exercise of such choice by an individual. Further, there was no physical location for any of the schools. Centers of excellence came up in one place in a certain age to appear in another where conditions were conducive. To illustrate, the province of Ferghana[1] in Central Asia has been the home for many Muslim jurists from different schools and even for specialists in traditions.

The judge or the qāḍī, though appointed by the rulers, was more like the head of an arbitration tribunal. This was especially true in civil matters. In certain instances this judge may have been paid a fee by the litigants to settle matters between them. In matters where the coercive power of the government or the ruler was needed, the qāḍī acted as the judicial arm of the government. The government also applied other rules sometimes, rules that had been developed

---

[1]Now split up between Uzbekistan, Kyrghysistan and others.

under the methodology of *siyāsah*, which in turn was developed by the jurists for this purpose.

There was no concept of the state in the sense of a "legal person" owning territory. Jurisdiction extended to the area where this law was applicable. The concept of the Ummah or community of Muslims governed this. It was more like a free system. Thus, to mention one case, the land over which this law prevailed was not "owned" by anyone as, for example, in the case of the British monarch who owned everything. Ownership could be exercised by anyone if he worked on the land and "revived" it by cultivation or construction. Such ownership lasted if the land was kept in the state of "revival." Ownership could be lost if the land was abandoned for some time. To mention another case, the wealth of the treasury was assumed to be owned jointly by the individuals who composed the Ummah.[2] There was a government run by the ruler or Imām minus the concept of the legal personality, that is, no legal person owned the territory.

As the law belonged to the schools, no ruler codified it. Even where such attempts were made the law was presented as an organised version of the law developed by the schools. One outstanding example is the *Fatāwā 'Ālamgiri*, which was developed on the instructions of the Moghul ruler Awrangzeb Alamgir, but it remained Ḥanafite law. As a large number of opinions may prevail within a school, the school acknowledged this variety, but at any one time the law to be followed was issued by the school in the form of preferred opinions in books that were often called *mukhtaṣars* or "the black-letter law," if you like. This is what the people, the jurists and judges were supposed to follow. A much later document called the *Majallat al-Aḥkam al-'Adliyyah* (18th Century) tried to give a new version of the "black-letter law," but it still was law of the Ḥanafī school. This does not mean that the government did not undertake codification of any kind. Short

---

[2]The rules followed by the schools show that the *bayt al-māl* or the "treasury" was in the "joint-ownership" of the Ummah.

codes were issued by governments, especially by the Ottomans and the Mughals, in the form of *qānūn'nāmahs* and *firmāns*. These have been explained elsewhere by the present author where he has also shown how they lock into the larger legal system.[3]

The binding force of the law arose not through the coercive power of a state, there being no state as stated, but through a system of voluntary acceptance and internalization. This is the true power of this law.[4] Those who dream of undoing the "authority" of the schools of Islamic law do not understand the nature of this law. This authority cannot be undone. The reason is that this authority is driven by the Qur'ān and the Sunnah and operates through the people themselves who are represented by their schools.

The features mentioned above show that Islamic law was developed by private persons on the basis of the texts of the Qur'ān and the Sunnah, absorbing in the process all good things in other systems if they were found compatible. The law was developed on the basis of choices exercised by the people, who voluntarily brought their disputes before a *qāḍī*, who acted more often than not as an arbitrator accepted by both parties. Of course, he was nominated by the ruler. The law was not developed by the government, or a state, but by schools of law formed by the people. No need was, therefore, felt for codification by the government. Finally, the binding force of this law was based on voluntary acceptance and internalization of their faith.

---

[3]See generally Imran Ahsan Khan Nyazee, *Theories of Islamic Law: The Methodology of Ijtihād* (Islamabad: Federal Law House, 2007).

[4]The term "Islamic State of Medina" is used by many to refer to the system set up by the Prophet (pbuh) at Medina. The word state in such writings does not mean al "legal person," but the government set up by the Prophet (pbuh) for the Muslim Ummah. State as a "legal person" is a complex concept that is not acknowledged by Islamic law as such. Those interested in the jurisprudence behind this discussion may refer to Imran Ahsan Khan Nyazee, *Corporations in Islam* (Islamabad: Federal Law House, 2007).

It is these features that will enable this law to spring into action at the international level with the help of modern technology. As this law has never been bound to a single location or territory, the opportunity provided by modern technology will enable this law to reemerge on the world scene as a true law for all mankind. This is what this brief book is about.

The present international law, following the Treaty of Westphalia, is based on the model presented by Islamic law since its birth. The existing international law has however been genetically modified for other reasons and purposes. To understand what we mean here, it is necessary to look at what is meant by "the existing international law." We have to go into some known details about international law as everyone does not study it. After describing international law briefly, as it is viewed by its experts, we will indicate what we mean by the Islamic model.

CHAPTER 2

THE ORIGIN AND RISE OF INTERNATIONAL LAW AND THE ISLAMIC MODEL

> A people is first conquered when
> it acquiesces to a foreign
> vocabulary, a foreign conception
> of what is law, especially
> international law.
>
> Carl Schmitt

In this chapter our aim is to elaborate the meaning of international law so as to show that it is based entirely on the European model that emerged after the Treaty of Westphalia in 1648 as well as the rise of modern states. Just before the emergence of the European model of states, the Islamic model based on a large number of Islamic lands and sultanates had worked on the basis of a uniform law that applied in different variations through the schools of law that represented different facets of the same legal system.

it is very difficult to believe that the European model had not been influenced by the then prevailing Islamic model. The European using colonization and brutal force gradually imposed its own model on the rest of the world, especially the colonies that were given independence later. In this model, the legal principles followed by the present international law are those of Western civilization, in particular those of the civil law prevailing in Europe.

Islamic law that had once operated as international law in a large part of the then known world was systematically and intentionally kept out. consequently, not a single principle of this vibrant law has been included in the prevailing international law. Although Muslims represent almost one-third of the entire world population today, lawmaking at the United Nations has been designed in such a way that Muslim nations cannot insist on the inclusion of their laws within the multilateral agreements and international conventions.

In the present chapter, we will attempt an explanation of the two models though an elaboration of the meaning of "international law."

2.1   Defining International Law

Our purpose here is not to study international, but some detail becomes unavoidable. The study of international law begins by facing a variety of terms with related meanings. Some of these terms represent ideas or concepts that are no longer current or have become obsolete. The terms are: "international law," "law of nations," "public international law," "private international law," "universal international law," "general international law," "regional international law," "particular international law," "international morality," "international comity," "regimes," and "civilized states." All these terms help in understanding and refining the meaning of modern international law, but in some ways they hinder such understanding. It is, therefore, essential to shed some of these terms before an attempt is made to define international law in earnest. We will begin by clarifying a few of these terms, while others will be dealt with through the definitions presented.

2.1.1   International Law as the Law of Nations

Today, the term "law of nations" and "international law" are not synonymous, but at some stage in history they were. "Law of nations" is the older term for the rules governing relations between the people of different lands. In French it is called *"droit de gens,"* while in German, Dutch, Scandinavian and Slavic languages the older terminology is still in use: "Völkerrecht," "Volkenrecht," and so on.[5] It can be traced back to the Roman concept of *jus gentium* (law for other nations) as distinguished from the *jus civile* (law for Romans), and is to be found in the writings of Cicero.[6] The word "nations" in this term does not mean "states," because states that are entities with a legal personality had not come into existence as yet; they came into existence in the sixteenth or seventeenth century. With the rise of the states, the terminology started shifting meanings, and jurists like Bentham maintained that *jus gentium* was no more than "the mutual transactions between sovereigns,"[7] in other words a narrow concept. In contrast, the term *jus inter gentes* was considered much wider and conveyed the meaning of "law between the peoples" or the body of treaty law. It was this term that Bentham translated to mean "international law." The terms "Völkerrecht" and "Volkenrecht," mentioned above, apparently identify this wider meaning.

As compared to this, in Islamic law, the term *siyar* (relations with non-Muslims) is defined by al-Sarakhsī as "the strategy of Muslims in dealing with the polytheists of the *dār al-ḥarb* (enemy territory), those among them with whom there is a truce, those seeking safe-custody, those who are the *ahl al-dhimmah* (those under Muslim authority on the basis of a contract) and those who are apostates."[8] The focus in this meaning is on individuals and their faith, that is, "peoples," and not on sovereigns. A study of

---

[5] Peter Malanczuk, *Akehurst's Modern Introduction to International Law*, 7th ed. (New York: Routledge, 1997), 1.

[6] Akehurst citing Cicero, *De officiis*, lib. III, 17, 69. ibid.

[7] Jeremy Bentham, *An Introduction to the Principles of Morals and Legislation* (Oxford: Clarendon Press, 1907), 327.

[8] Shams al-A'immah Sarakhsī, *Kitāb al-Mabsūṭ*, ed. Abū 'Abd Allāh Ismā'īl al Shāfi'ī, 30 vols. (Beirut: Dār al-Kutub al-'Ilmiyyah, 2001), vol. 10, 3.

siyar shows that it is a law based on treaties concluded right from the birth of Islam.

The definition given by al-Sarakhsī focuses only on those regions that are at war with the Muslim lands. It talks about: how war is to be waged and truce concluded; how visas are to be granted and trade carried out with the enemy; and how the lands and other matters of governance are to be carried out in these areas. Scholars have considered this to be all that Islamic law has to say about international law. This definition does not talk about, for example, how Egypt would deal with the Centrals Asian states or with Syria and Iraq for that matter, and how all these regions will deal and trade with Indonesia and Malaysia in the distant east. The definition does not talk about wars within Muslim lands and regions or trade between them. It also does not talk about matters of personal law or the rights of the children and the poor of these regions. What we are implying here is that to understand the internal law of Islam, one has to examine the laws that deal with and manage the dār al-ḥarb, and those that manage matters within the dār al-Islam.

Accordingly, the term *jus inter gentes* comes much closer to the meaning of *siyar*, as used in Islamic law. The term *siyar* does not carry within it the meaning of states rather it conveyes the meaning of treaties between peoples. Further, *siyar* was a law that dealt not only with peoples, but also with individuals in certain cases, as in the case of apostates and those seeking visas.

Today, however, "law of nations" is defined as "the body of legal rules binding on states in their international dealings with other states."[9]

The word "states" when it was incorporated into the definition of international law also brought with it the concept of "civilized states." Thus, Oppenheim, a highly respected authority in international law, defined international law as follows: "Law

---

[9]Ray August, *Public International Law: Text, Cases and Readings*, 1st ed. (New Jersey: Prentice Hall, 1995), 2.

of Nations or International Law is the name for the body of customary and treaty rules which are considered legally binding by civilized States in their intercourse with each other."[10] If we replace the term "civilized states" by the term "Muslim lands," it will become obvious what we mean by Islamic law as international law: "civilized states" means exactly what we mean by "dār al-Islām." The powerful caliphate of the Ottoman times that flourished a few centuries preceding the Treaty of Westphalia, a caliphate that was acknowledged by many as "civilized Muslim lands" extending up to Indonesia must have exerted a powerful influence over the Western model of international law.

The term civilized has been criticized by writers as being demeaning, and pertaining to the days of colonization. Article 38 of the ICJ uses the term as do all writers and courts. It has been maintained by others that "civilized should not be seen as a demeaning term; the Statute is merely referring to states that have reached an advanced state of legal development."[11] It appears that "civilized" meant that those who were not civilized could be conquered, brutalized and deprived of their resources without bothering about "civilized" morality. In any case, this definition treats states as the only subjects of international law. In this context, states that are "not civilized" may be referred to as the "dār al-ḥarb" if we compare early Western international states law with Islamic law as international law.

---

[10]L. Oppenheim, *International Law*, vol. 1, 8th ed. (1970), 4–5. Earlier, in 1890, Hall had said: "International law consists in certain rules of conduct which modern *civilised states* regard as being binding on them in their relations with one another with a force comparable in nature and degree to that binding the conscientious person to obey the laws of the country, and which they also regard as being enforceable by appropriate means in case of infringement." W. E. Hall, *A Treatise on International Law*, 3rd ed. (Oxford: Clarendon Press, 1890).

[11] Anthony Aust, *Handbook of International Law* (Cambridge: Cambridge University Press, 2005), 8. This is worse than saying civilized.

International law today is considered to regulate the relations between states, institutions and individuals as well in certain cases. The change took place gradually, however, certain writers argue that the core meaning of the term international law still applies to states. Bentham first used the term "international law," when he translated the Latin term *jus inter gentes* (literally "the law governing relations between peoples"), and since then the term has been confined to this core meaning. Writers like Akehurst have argued that international law still applies, in reality, to states. "The prevailing positivist doctrine of the nineteenth century and first half of the twentieth century held that only states could be subjects of international law, in the sense of enjoying international legal personality and being capable of possessing international rights and duties, including the right to bring international claims."[12] This approach was adopted consistently even though with time certain institutions were recognized as having rights under international law. Later on, many intergovernmental organizations were recognized. Nevertheless, such recognition comes through treaties between states and these institutions are really based in the territories of such states. The learned writer acknowledges that while definitions of international law have started including subjects other than states in the meaning, international law is primarily law that governs the relationship of states.

As late as 1927, the Permanent Court of International Justice upheld the same concept, when it was called upon to decide a dispute between France and Turkey. The court tried to lay down the parameters of international law in the following words:

> International law governs relations between independent states. The rules of law binding upon states therefore emanate from their own free will as expressed in conventions or by usages

---

[12]Malanczuk, *Akehurst's Introduction to International Law*, 1.

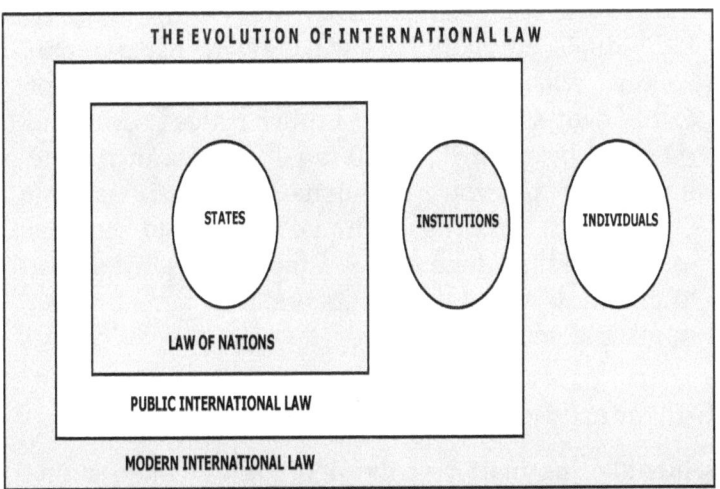

generally accepted as expressing principles of law and established in order to regulate the relations between these co-existing independent communities or with a view to the achievement of common aims.[13]

Even more recents writings exhibit the same emphasis on states being the real subjects of international law:

> "International law" is a strict term of art, connoting that system of law whose primary function it is to regulate the relations of states with one another. As states have formed organisations of themselves, it has come also to be concerned with international organisations and an increasing concern with them must follow from the trend which we are now witnessing towards the integration of the community of states. And because states are composed of

---

[13]*The Lotus case*, PCLJ Ser A, No 10 (1927).

individuals and exist primarily to serve the needs of individuals, international law has always had a certain concern with the relations of the individual, if not to his own state, at least to other states ...even the relations between the individual and his own state have come to involve questions of international law .... Nevertheless, international law is and remains essentially a law for states and thus stands in contrast to what international lawyers are accustomed to call municipal law.[14]

2.1.2   Modern International Law

Consequently, the matter of the definition of international law really rests on who are the true subjects of international law: states alone or institutions and individuals as well. A change in thinking really began with the Nuremberg War Crimes Tribunal in 1946 when it raised questions about the international obligations of individuals.[15]   This could be one reason why the Universal Declaration of Human Rights, 1948 suggested the possibility of individual international rights.

Once the the United Nations was established it was followed by the creation of a number of other supra-national organisations.

---

[14]C. Parry and M. Sorensen (ed), *Manual of Public International Law* (London: Macmillan, 1968).

[15]"The Nuremberg and Tokyo Tribunals set up by the victorious Allies after the close of the Second World War were a vital part of this process. Many of those accused were found guilty of crimes against humanity and against peace and were punished accordingly. It was a recognition of individual responsibility under international law without the usual interposition of the state and has been reinforced with the establishment of the Yugoslav and Rwanda War Crimes Tribunals in the mid-1990s and the International Criminal Court in 1998." Malcolm N. Shaw, *International Law*, 6th ed. (Cambridge: Cambridge University Press, 2008), 46.

The determination of their status within the community of nation states became extremely important. In 1949 the International Court of Justice was asked by the General Assembly of the United Nations for its opinion on matters arising out of the assassination of a UN representative in Jerusalem. In its judgment the court declared that the United Nations Organisation had a legal personality and was a subject of international law. Thus, it was capable of possessing international rights and duties, and had the legal capacity to maintain its rights by bringing international claims.[16] It was gradually acknowledged that modern international law has a wider role to play and its subjects include states, intergovernmental institutions and even individuals in some cases. The definition of international law began to change in the writings of specialists or publicists as they are called. The famous Hersch Lauterpacht defined it as follows:

> International law is the body of rules of conduct, enforceable by external sanction, which confer rights and impose obligations primarily, though not exclusively, upon sovereign states and which owe their validity both to the consent of states as expressed in

---

[16] *Reparation for Injuries Suffered in the Service of the United Nations case,* ICJ 1949, at p. 174 of Report. See also Ibid., 47: "International organisations have now been accepted as possessing rights and duties of their own and a distinctive legal personality. The International Court of Justice in 1949 delivered an Advisory Opinion in which it stated that the United Nations was a subject of international law and could enforce its rights by bringing international claims, in this case against Israel following the assassination of Count Bernadotte, a United Nations official. Such a ruling can be applied to embrace other international institutions, like the International Labour Organisation and the Food and Agriculture Organisation, which each have a judicial character of their own. Thus, while states remain the primary subjects of international law, they are now joined by other non-state entities, whose importance is likely to grow even further in the future."

custom and treaties and to the fact of the existence of an international community of states and individuals. In that sense international law may be defined more briefly (though perhaps less usefully), as the law of the international community.[17]

Ray August, defining international law, says: "International Law is the body of rules and norms that regulates activities carried on outside the legal boundaries of nations. In particular, it regulates three international relationships: (1) those between states and states, (2) those between states and persons, and (3) those between persons and persons."[18] This definition is quite adequate when the subjects of modern international law are taken into account. The figure above, inspired by Ray August, distinguishes the meaning of modern law from other meanings.

Starke defines it as follows: "International law may be defined as that body of law which is composed for its greater part of the principles and rules of conduct which states feel themselves bound to observe, and therefore, do commonly observe in their relations with each other, and which includes also:

(*a*) the rules of law relating to the functioning of international institutions or organisations, their relations with each other, and their relations with states and individuals; and

(*b*) certain rules of law relating to individuals and non-state entities so far as the rights or duties of such individuals and non-state entities are the concern of the international community."[19]

---

[17]Hersch Lauterpacht, *Collected Papers,* vol. 1 (Cambridge: Cambridge University Press, 1970).

[18]August, *Public International Law,* 1.

[19]He then adds that this definition goes beyond the traditional definition of international law as a system composed solely of rules

Conway Henderson provides a precise definition with which we will end the discussion of the definition of international law. He says: "International law is the collection of rules and norms that states and other actors feel an obligation to obey in their mutual relations and commonly do obey."[20] The words "other actors" obviously include intergovernmental bodies and individuals.

2.1.3   Can Islamic Law Recognize States and Institutions as Subjects

A state is a legal person that owns a particular territory. This gives this legal person exclusive control over everything that exists within that territory, and it also gives it the right to deal with whatever exists outside this territory. The Muslim concept of the "ummah" does not have these features, as that is a mere community, or an association of persons that does not have legal personality. It is more like a large number of partners who jointly own a particular territory and whatever has come under its authority.

As the modern state owns its territory and everything within it, anything that is done within its territory has to be done with the permission of this legal person, even acts of worship. This inserts a wedge between the individual and his Creator. In other words, the individual can communicate with his Creator (at least when speaking out loud) only with the permission of the state. Only those things can be done that are permitted by the state. Thus, if the Qur'ān says, "Verily, the *ḥukm* (command or law) belongs to Allah, and no one but Allah," it cannot be applied directly. We leave the reader to ponder over this.

---

governing the relations between states only. I. A. Shearer, *Starke's International Law*, 11th ed. (London: Butterworths, 1995), 3.

[20]Conway W. Henderson, *Understanding International Law*, 1st ed. (West Sussex: John Wiley & Sons, 2010), 5.

The reason that this concept of legal person or state cannot be compatible with Islamic law is that this law revolves around an *ahd* or covenant that a human being has with the Creator; a fictitious legal person cannot have such a covenant with the Creator of human beings.[21] The only way that the legal person, state or a corporation can be accepted by Islamic law is when such a legal person is legally assumed to be the "agent" of the group behind it, whether this is the ummah, the shareholders or even an individual. In other words, the state cannot own the property; it belongs to the ummah and is owned by it. The corporation cannot exclusively own its assets, they belong to the shareholders as if it were a very large partnership.[22]

The only subjects that Islamic law will recognize then are individuals and groups, even when such groups are called peoples and nations. Institutions, organisations and associations will be seen as true agents of these peoples or groups and not independent persons in their own right. Muslims will, of course, agree or disagree with the statements made under this section, but that is the whole idea. At least, they should think about the problem. If they do not see a problem here without discussion or arguments, then there is a problem with their status as Muslims. What we are swaying here is that if, for example, the United States of America drops atomic bombs over Hiroshima and Nagasaki, the American people cannot turn around and say that it was the "state" that is guilty of such an attrocity, and we as a people are innocent or that we too are victims of this "state." Islamic law will tell you that the "state" has no real existence, it is merely your agent, and you as a people are directly responsible and accountable for the acts of your agent the "state."

For an understanding of the meaning of international law, from the perspective of Islamic law, there are many other topics

---

[21] For the details, see Imran Ahsan Khan Nyazee, *Islamic Legal Maxims* (Islamabad: Federal Law House, 2013).

[22] For a very detailed discussion, see Nyazee, *Partnership in Islam,*

like the subject-matter and scope of international law, whether
international law is really law, what functions it performs and so
on. It is not our purpose to pursue those ideas here. We may,
therefore, move straight to the origins of international law.

2.2 The Origins of International Law

The idea of international law is usually linked with the term *jus
gentium*, which was first used by Marcus Tullius Cicero (106–
43 B.C.).[23] Cicero did not clearly define *jus gentium*, but he did
refer "to lesser societies made up of gentes, or those formed into
cities."[24] He pointed out the ancients desired two kinds of law:
"the law of nations and civil law—the former ideally being a part
of the latter."[25] In other words, *jus gentitum* or the law meant for
lesser societies was actually a part of the *jus civilie* or the law of
civilized people. The idea of "civilized societies," thus, appears
to have emerged from here, and is found in legal documents
even today.[26] There are others who link the idea of international
law to the rules of the ancient civilizations of China, the Greek
city-states, the Indian states, and Persia in the dealings of these
entities with outsiders. A favorite point of other writers is that the

---

[23]Rafael Domingo, *The New Global Law* (Cambridge: Cambridge
University Press, 2010), 6.

[24]Ibid., 7. Wolff called *gentes* "the set of people who live in association
in a city. These people are to be thought of as singular, free persons
living in a state of nature. Under the influence of Hobbes, he takes
as his point of departure a state of nature that he applies as much
to persons as to *civitates*. Departing from that English philosopher,
however, he considers it a nature of moral character." Ibid., 27.

[25]Ibid., 7.

[26]Gaius spoke of *jus gentium* at the beginning of his *Institutes* and
contrasted it with *jus civile*. He said that civilized peoples—that is,
those organized according to law and custom—govern themselves
partly by their own law and partly by the law common to all people.
Ibid., 9.

Mesopotamian communities concluded treaties as early as 3100 B.C.[27] We have, however, given our own suggestion of "civilized states" being the equivalent of dar al-Islam.

2.2.1   Early Developments Summarized

The development of international law is traced as follows:

1. **Collapse of the Roman Empire and the Rise of Christendom:** With the disappearance of Roman rule, and the rise of the Islamic Empire, Europe lost its unity under an effective central authority. The Medieval Age (476–1350 CE) overtook Europe, bringing in its wake a mishmash of entities, including manor estates, duchies, walled cities, monasteries, and fiefdoms ruled by kings. As for unity, there existed only a loose order of overlapping authorities. This authority was vested in the Roman Catholic Church and the Holy Roman Empire. Together, these overlapping authorities headed a ramshackle society in Western Europe known as Christendom.[28] At this time, the Muslim lands existed as a highly inter-linked and well knit body of territories and peoples following an international law called Islamic law.

2. **The Legacy of Rome:** Rome left behind the important legacy of the Justinian Code, the apex of Roman law compiled between 528 and 534 CE. It is said that law was rediscovered by Europeans centuries later, and it set the basis for the code laws of European states, other than that of England. It also imparted the idea that if Rome could have a special law governing relations with the peoples living on the periphery

---

[27]Henderson, *Understanding International Law*, 9; see also Gideon Boas, *Public International Law: Contemporary Principles and Perspectives* (Cheltenham, UK: Edward Elgar Publishing Limited, 2012), 6–7.
[28]Henderson, *Understanding International Law*, 10.

of their empire, then Europeans might have law among independent kings. *Jus gentium* no longer applied to the inferior barbarians outside the boundaries of the Roman Empire but to the rudimentary "civilized" states of Europe. Here we may recall that the Justinian Code had been lost and was rediscovered at a time when the Islamic civilization was at its zenith. Is it possible that the glosses written on this code were influenced by the all-powerful Islamic law that dominated the world scene at that time? Research from this perspective may turn up new facts.

3. **The Dream of a Christian Kingdom in Europe:** The early efforts to establish a Christian empire were made by Charlemagne (742–814 CE). About 150 years after Charlemagne's death, the Holy Roman Empire tried to pull his empire back together. Usually governed by a German emperor, with the approval of a Roman Chatholic Church. This in itself shows the tremendous influence the dominant Islamic empire must have exerted. The Holy Roman Empire existed from 962 until 1806. Napoleon Bonaparte dissolved it in 1806 after the Empire had been considerably diminished. Voltaire (1694–1778), the famous French philosopher, denouncing the Empire in an artifice, reportedly said that it was "neither Holy, Roman, nor an Empire."

4. **Reformation, Renaissance and the Rise of States:** The Reformation devastated the Catholic religious monopoly over Europe. This period started in 1517. Martin Luther, a Professor of Theology, began the reform movement by initiating a debate over the corruption and doctrine of the Roman Chatholic Church. Many sects of the Protestant faith were created, which in turn led to the division of Europe into Catholic and Protestant states. It led ultimately to the Thirty Year War (1618–48).

The Renaissance also contributed to the making of strong kings and countries by promoting commerce, art, science, and a new work ethic. A new merchant class, or bourgeoisie, arose that could now offer taxes and loans to kings enabling them to develop professional armies equipped with latest military equipment. The kings brought the nobles under their control and on gaining strength stopped acknowledging the authority of the Holy roman Empire. Private business law, known as merchant law, was also developed. We need not mention here the role that the Islamic civilization had to play not only in the Renaissance and Reformation but also in the development of the law merchant, the lex mercatoria.

5. **The Thirty Year War and the Treaty of Westphalia:** Religious and political causes led to the Thirty Year War. Ultimately, the 1648 Peace of Westphalia ended the Thirty Year War. Underlying it was the thinking of Jean Bodin (1530–1596) that *kings and their states should enjoy their sovereignty as legal equals and be able to act independently of each other. A critical rule that emerged was that states could not interfere with one another in internal matters for religious or other reasons.* Without the guidance of the Emperor's authority, sovereign kings accepted new rules on how to deal with one another.[29] The rules based on the customary practices of European states and the writings of philosophers led to the creation of the new European society, a society that had been forming before 1648 and continues to develop today, but now on a global scale.[30] Research must be undertaken to determine the extent to which this new European society owes its development to the Islamic civilization and to Islamic international law.

---

[29]Malanczuk, *Akehurst's Introduction to International Law*, 10.
[30]Henderson, *Understanding International Law*, 11.

Malanczuk has recorded certain important events that show the development of international law after the Treaty of Westphalia:[31]

- **The French Revolution of 1789** challenged the basis of the existing system by advocating the ideas of freedom and self-determination of people.

- **The Vienna Congress of 1815** made the second attempt in history to create a collective security system and was somewhat more successful as compared to the earlier efforts.

- **Paris Peace Treaty of 1856.** The Crimean War, in which Russia was defeated by the alliance of France and Great Britain, supported by Piedmont-Sardinia and Turkey, ended with the Paris Peace Treaty of 1856.

- **The Balkan Wars of 1912/13.** The Berlin Congress of 1878, failed to solve the Balkan problems and the struggle of European powers over the distribution of spoils emerging in the Orient from the disintegration of the Ottoman Empire culminated in the Balkan Wars of 1912/13, bringing the Concert of Europe to its end.

- **Colonization began in certain lands.** European expansion abroad in the interest of trade and commerce was promoted in England, the Netherlands and France by ruthless profit-making companies, such as the British East India Company, enjoying privileges which permitted them to perform state functions in overseas territories.

- **European nations recognized certain empires.** The Europeans recognized the Mogul Empire in India, the Ottoman Empire, Persia, China, Japan, Burma, Siam (renamed Thailand in 1939) and Ethiopia as established

---

[31]Malanczuk, *Akehurst's Introduction to International Law*, 11-15.

political entities, but they were aware that these states did not play a major role in global affairs. By the Paris Peace Treaty of 1856 Turkey was even expressly admitted (as the first non-Christian nation) to the Concert of Europe.

- **Some nations resisted colonization, but others could not.** The Ottoman Empire found it difficult to accept the Christian nations it was confronted with at its borders in Europe as equal and insisted on its superiority. Similarly, China, "the empire in the centre of the earth," preferred isolation to contact with foreigners, from whom nothing more than tribute was expected to be due.[32] The Moghul Empire did not display such wisdom.

- **Belief in the superiority of the "white man."** By about 1880 Europeans had subdued most of the non-European states, which was interpreted in Europe as conclusive proof of the inherent superiority of the white man, and the international legal system became a white man's club, to which non-European states would be admitted only if they produced evidence that they were "civilized."

---

[32]When Britain requested in 1793 that China accept a British envoy, the Emperor responded as follows: "As to your entreaty to send one of your nationals to be accredited to my Celestial Court and to be in control of your country's trade with China, this request is contrary to all usage of my dynasty and cannot possibly be entertained .... Our ceremonies and code of laws differ so completely from your own that, even if your Envoy were able to acquire the rudiments of our civilization, you could not possibly transplant our manners and customs to your alien soil.... Swaying the wide world, I have but one aim in view, namely, to maintain a perfect governance and to fulfill the duties of the state.... I set no value on objects strange or ingenious, and have no use for your country's manufactures." As quoted in Malanczuk, *Akehurst's Introduction to International Law,* 12-13.

- **The Monroe Doctrine and American international law.**
  The Monroe Doctrine, which stated that further efforts by
  European nations to colonize land or interfere with states
  in North or South America would be viewed as acts of
  aggression, requiring U.S. intervention, led to independent
  developments. South American states attempted to protect
  themselves against foreign intervention and European
  dominance by formulating a new regional American
  international law.

- **Resistance by Japan finally put an end to the invincibility
  of the "white man."** Japan had modernized by adopting
  Western technology and ways. Finally, the end of white rule
  and the complex process of decolonization in Asia was then
  brought forward by Japanese aggression and initial victories
  in the Second World War, which helped to destroy the myth
  of the invincibility of the European colonial masters.

The crux of the matter is that the modern system of
international law is a product of the last four hundred years,
and coincides with the emergence of modern states having legal
personality.[33] It is said that it grew out of the usages and practices
of modern European states in their commercial intercourse and

---

[33] According to Gideon Boas, "This development of the concept of the
nation state increasingly caused states to be seen as 'permanently
existing, corporate entities in their own right, separate from the
rulers who governed them at any given time.' One of the key
concepts to come out of the development of the nation state was
that the law of nations only governed inter-state relations, and that
rulers were free to 'govern as they please' within their state. This can
be seen as the beginnings of the concept of state sovereignty. This
exciting development in international law, reflecting a significant
evolution in the rights of states within the sphere of international
law, has soured increasingly over the past two centuries. The idea
of the complete equality of states (no matter how large or small) in
international law became lost during the nineteenth century 'under

communications. It was influenced to some extent by the writers and jurists of the sixteenth, seventeenth, and eighteenth centuries, who first formulated some of its most fundamental tenets.[34] The law remains tinged with concepts such as national and territorial sovereignty, and the perfect equality and independence of states, that owe their force to political theories underlying the modern European state system. Weaker states were compelled to join this system, after decolonization, due to economic or other pressures, because they had nowhere else to turn to.

The legal and political developments listed above are important for understanding the development of international law, however, it is necessary to list some underlying causes. Conway quoting Martin Wight says that international law began with the sixteenth-century debate in Spain over the status of "Indians" in the Americas. Did Spain have the right to absorb much of the Americas in the western hemisphere into their empire by refusing to recognize any rights on the part of the indigenous peoples to their own lands? The Spanish and other Europeans came to view the Americas as *terra nullius*, that is, land belonging to no one and subject to European conquest. The interests of the indigenous peoples were simply brushed aside.[35] In reality, the same approach was adopted with respect to all "uncivilized"

---

the influence of the diametrically opposed idea of the hegemony of the great Powers.' The same sentiment is reflected in the twentieth-century revolt against massive human rights violations committed by the leadership of states against their own citizens. Nonetheless, the principle of state sovereignty was and remains the fundamental principle upon which modern international law is based, reflected in the UN Charter, representing the now paramount importance of the principle of sovereignty in international law." Boas, *Public International Law*, 9-10 (footnotes omitted).

[34]*Cf.* Malanczuk's view below.

[35]Henderson, *Understanding International Law*, 9-10. "The territory of Europe would thus become a theater of war (*theatrum belli*), whereas non-European territory would be called *res nullius* and therefore

people whose lands were colonized. All this was done to meet the commercial needs of European nations. The easiest way to do this was by grabbing territory belonging to other nations. International law, then, began as an understaning between the European nations on how the wealth of other lands will be shared. We have already indicated a probable basis of International law, but the following may also be kept in mind.

1. The primary need for international law is the security of transactions related to banking, commerce and international trade.

2. In fact, it was the rise of the commercial classes that led to the development of international law. The role of these classes in the wars in Europe and in the first and second world wars bears ample testimony of this fact. Most wars have been the by-product of economic domination. The East-India Company, it may be recalled, started as a commercial enterprise.

3. These classes created the modern corporation with an independent legal personality. The same model was imposed on the kingdoms of Europe, which were organized around the concept of legal personality for carving out modern states as independent entities.

4. The concept of state was then developed on the basis of territory and it was this ownership from which many legal rules emerged.

2.2.2   The Possible Influence of the Islamic System

In the above paragraphs, we have stated that modern international law was confined to Europe in the early stages, and the European

---

open to unrestricted occupation by European states." Domingo, *The New Global Law*, 25.

states were more like an international society that carried out colonial campaigns in the rest of the world. It was only after the first World War that international law really began taking the shape of an "international" law. After the second World War, the smaller states in Asia and Africa joined for one reason or the other, and this gave this European law a true international character. It is, therefore, natural for Western writers not to acknowledge the role played by the Islamic Empire and by Islamic law in the development of international law.

Some Western writers, or publicists as they are called, do mention the 00000kkexistence of the Islamic legal system, but only as a passing reference.[36] One reason for this is that Muslims have been engaged in the discussion whether Imam Muḥammad al-Shaybānī, the author of *al-Siyar al-Kabīr*, was the real "father" of international law or whether it was Hugo Grotius. The matter, in our view, has to be examined from a different perspective.

Islamic law, the law of *siyar* in particular, had detailed rules about *jus ad bellum* (law to begin war, often understood as war for a just cause) and *jus in bello* (law of war), the basis for which is found in the military campaigns of the Prophet (pbuh). Nevertheless, these rules were followed unilaterally by Muslims and not by non-Muslims. The brutality exhibited by the crusaders, in violation of all human norms, in Palestine is a matter of recorded history. Further, when the Islamic empire was at its zenith, Europe and other areas, except China, were more like "uncivilized" nations. Thus, the rules framed by Muslims for the conduct of war were not followed by the rest of the world. Consequently, Islamic law cannot be said to be international law in this sense.

Islamic law, however, was international law in another sense. The Islamic empire ultimately stretched from Spain at one end to Malaysia, and Indonesia at the other or from Africa to Sicily

---

[36]See, e.g. Shaw, *International Law*, Malanczuk, *Akehurst's Introduction to International Law*, and more recently Rafael Domingo, *The New Global Law* (Cambridge: Cambridge University Press, 2010).

and certain areas of Europe. In the later centuries, this empire was not really one nation, but was composed of many sultanates, or countries, some of which were empires in their own right, like the Moghul empire in India. The position of the Khalifah became more like the head of an international organization whose approval had to be sought for validating the rule of the sultans. In other words, there were multiple sultanates in this huge area, and some of the sultans were extremely powerful.

The above map shows the Islamic world at the time the Treaty of Westphalia was concluded. It shows a large number of states. Islamic law applied uniformly across this huge area in every state, with variations according to the school followed. It shows three empires, but they all recognized and owed allegaince to the Khalifah. Trade was carried out among the multiple sultanates on the basis of Islamic law, and many other types of laws were also applied uniformly. When there were wars among the sultanates, the laws of war were also followed to the extent applicable to Muslims.[37] Muslim traders spread all over the world and influenced the rules of trade and commerce. The word *aval* (indorsement) is still used in France for the Islamic *ḥawālah*. The rulers in Europe learned much from the Islamic legal and other systems. Reformation and Renaissance in Europe were also the result of Muslim works in the arts, law and the sciences. Many universtities established in England and Europe followed the model of the *madāris* established in Spain. Islamic law also had a direct impact on Europe, especially during the days of Sulaymān Ālishān. Acknowledging this, Joseph Schacht, the well known Orientalist, said that this law was "the swiftest law in Europe."

The facts stated clearly indicate a legal system that prevailed over much of the known world in its time, and operated in a much more effective way than international law does even today, must have had a very deep impact on the development of the European international society or law. The reason is that the European civilization was in direct contact with this system at the time of the birth of its international law. In fact, this influence started much earlier.[38] Hinsley, among other thngs, has the following to say:

> So much was this so that the possibility arose that Europe would develop into a single theocracy on the lines of Islam when it had lost the political unity which Byzantium managed to preserve. ...But the Pope, like the Caliph, did not govern; and the law which he announced—the canon law—was not a law but a morality which recognized no distinction between the religious, political and social fields. ...Even so, the papal theocratic argument could not come to dominate political thought and practice in Europe to the extent

---

[37]For the details of this structure and the role of the Khalifah and sultans, see Nyazee, *Theories of Islamic Law*, 323-31.

[38]F. H. Hinsley, *Sovereignty* (Cambridge: Cambridge University Press, 1986), 54–56.

> that it dominated in the Islamic world. ...Muslims sometimes described the Pope as the Caliph of the Franks, as the Latins often confused the political status of the Caliph with the primarily ecclesiastic position of the Pope. In truth, however, the Pope could be only the Caliph of the Messiah. Nothing that he could do could prevent Emperors from regarding his claim to be more than this as what it was in fact—"a usurpation of an established imperial right to rule."[39]

The "Islamic model of international law" was thus visible for European "eyes" before they began creating their own model. It is, however, not the fault of Western publicists that this model is ignored in their writings. The fault lies with Muslim writers and countries who have yet to emerge from their "inferiority complex" acquired during colonization. Muslim scholars need to devote their energy to the discovery of the details of the Islamic model.

The population of the Muslims in the world is about to touch 2 billion, which is nearly one-third of the total population. In about another 50 years or less the Muslim population will be one-half or more of the total world population. It should be considered natural that some of the principles and fundamentals of this civilization will be taken into account by international law. Not a single principle, however, has been acknowledged in the numerous documents called declarations, treaties, conventions and protocols when these instruments now cover almost every aspect of human life, even very private matters. Only lipservice was paid to these principles in an arbitration case: *Libyan American Oil Company (LIAMCO) v. Government of the Libyan Arab Republic* (1977). Dr. Sobhi Mahmassani was the sole arbitrator so he brought in some discussion of a few principles of his own accord but without the principles having any bearing on the case.

---

[39]Ibid.

As stated, the norms of Islamic law have not been recognized in the prevalent international law, which is based on Anglo-American ideas and principles. The Muslim population of the world is on the rise and will soon surpass all others. This will compel the recognition and application of the principles of Islamic law. The international community will have to recognize these principles and apply them; there is no way that this can be avoided.

Islamic law has, with the rise of the modern state and the resulting colonization, been compelled to remain dormant for the last several centuries. The law must reemerge now in its proper role at the international level and prepare to make the contribution that Muslims require. It must recognize the transactions of the modern world and begin to pass them through the sieve of its sources, in order to see what can be "Islamized" and what cannot. The modern world with its rapid and complex means of communication now appears ready to witness the reemergence of this law. The growth of this law has remained stunted within the fold of the "state." It needs to reemerge in its free form on the world scene even if it is not acknowledged by international law and its institutions and even by the states.

CHAPTER 3

THE REEMERGENCE OF ISLAMIC LAW AT THE INTERNATIONAL LEVEL

Islamic law, which has been dormant for almost five centuries, must grow if it has to solve modern problems that are faced by all humanity in general and Muslims in particular. During these five centuries or more, the law has grown but in a negligible or insignificant manner. One main reason for this lack of growth has been the absence of a methodology that can support the required growth. The second has been colonization due to which Muslims have had to deal with the greed and brutality of their then colonial masters. The third and most important reason, however has been the rise of the state as a legal person. It is, therefore, significant that the arrival of the British in India coincides with the rise of modern states in Europe.

The last two reasons, mentioned above, arrested the growth of Islamic law. They took away the free environment in which the law could grow. The restrictive environment provided by the state prevented the free exchange of ideas. There was also no incentive for the exchange of such ideas as the state had monopolized all law making. This situation continues even after the end of colonization as it is now the state that has taken over all the functions of the colonial masters. In short, the natural environment in which Islamic law had grown in the first one thousand years of its existence has been taken away. This natural environment can now be restored with the shrinking of the world into a global village and with developments in modern technology and communications. It can be done without disturbing the existing structure of states and their authority.

In this chapter, we will address three major points. The first point will be about the difficulties that Islamic law is facing within the environment provided by modern states. The second will take up the explanation of what exactly we mean by the emergence or reemergence of Islamic law at the international level. The third topic is about the way this reemergence will begin, that is, what are those priority areas in which Islamic law can first contribute at the international level. We will first take up for discussion the hurdles in the face of the free growth of Islamic law.

3.1   The Hurdles Faced by Islamic Law With Respect to its Growth Within the Modern State

The state as an independent person is not owned by its citizens. It is the state that owns the citizens, just like it owns the territory under its jurisdiction as well as everything else that exists in that territory. The state makes its citizens work and contribute a part of their earnings to the state so that it can continue to perpetuate its existence. Any resources that the state allows its citizens to "own" and use can be taken back when the state needs them. In order to survive, the state defends itself against internal threats as well as against external dangers. The external goal of the state is survival, while the internal goal is growth. For these two goals, it makes the citizens strive and work to generate the resources that are sufficient for its survival and growth. These matters do not concern us here.

What does concern us here is that the state is a secular being. It can have no religion. The reason is that the state does not owe its birth to God, like man does. It cannot have the 'ahd or covenant with the Almighty that we have mentioned earlier. Further, as Hans Kelsen says, the state is the law. This law can only be driven by two goals: survival of the state and its growth. Any other law, with different goals, will be viewed as a threat by this state and its law. In addition to this, the state works hand in glove with the concept of democracy, which is also a secular concept. Its primary duty is to ensure equality. Consequently, it will try to give equal rights and opportunity even to those who will work against what the Almighty requires, and who might try to demolish Islamic law and eliminate it altogether. The only "religion" the state will tolerate is one that is practised within the confines of one's bedroom or living room, and is taken occasionally to church.

Islam, however, is not a "religion," it is a "deen" or a system. It does not know the difference between secular and religious, or the polical and religious, or Ceaser and the Pope. It has a complete law with a whole system of duties that cover every aspect of human life. It has come into this world to provide solutions to world problems, especially those of the poor. It will not "turn the other cheek," nor consider poverty a sin but will react with an appropriate and effective response. It is not driven by the goals of some legal person, but by the *maqāṣid al-sharī'ah* (objectives of the shari'ah) that the Almighty has determined for this law and for those who have faith in this law. A system with these purposes is naturally seen as hostile by the creature called the state, whichever state that might be. The state may be one with a Muslim majority or one with a Muslim minority. This law, with the system it visualizes, will be seen by all states as hostile.

The legal person called the state has given birth to many new kinds of legal persons that support its existence. The most formidable of these is the multinational corporation or the multinational enterprise, also called the transnational corporation. These beings have the ability to move resources worldwide and they have grown bigger, in certain cases, than many small countries. This form of the legal person is no longer in need of territory, but it does own its employees from whom it demands a fierce type of loyalty. It will survive, even if the modern states disintegrate and dissolve into small communities. As compared to the state, it does not have to protect territory; if one territory refuses to grant it a home another one will. Islamic law is up against this form of legal person too as it will always view this law as hostile.[40]

All this does not mean that Islam or Islamic law is against the idea of the state as a legal person, or even that of the corporation as a legal person. The requirement of Islamic law is that humans should ultimately bear all responsibility and be held liable for whatever the state or the corporation does. The only way this is possible is if the legal person is treated merely as an administrative tool or device, and is treated as an agent of the persons who own it. To illustrate a minor effect of this arrangement, we may notice the impact on those who direct the affairs of such agents who are legal persons. The officials of the state will lose all kinds of immunities from prosecution or litigation. They will be held personally accountable, unless the act they performed was purely for the Ummah and the community. In the same way, the concept of limited liability will have to be done away with and all the shareholders will be held liable for the debts and torts of the corporation, which is an agent of these shareholders.[41] We need not dwell on these issues here.

In the meantime, Islamic law needs a free environment for it to grow. This environment is not available to it within the confines of the state, whichever state this may be. The reason as already explained is that by inherent design the goals of the state cannot be in line with the goals of Islamic law. Making Islamic law subservient to a legal person, and restricting it within the confines of such a person, is detrimental to the growth of this law. This is like granting authority to one group of people to take over the goals of Islamic law. This group will always attempt to impose its own goals over the goals of Islamic law.

---

[40] At the time of writing this, the European Court of Justice has ruled that a Muslim female's services can be terminated by the corporation if she continues to wear the *hijāb*.

[41] Under Islamic law not secular law.

Islamic law developed by the state will always be viewed with suspicion and will be considered as restricted and subservient to the goals and purposes of the state. If the state is compelled or swayed by the majority in a country to change its laws to the Islamic form, then the first thing it will do is to focus on the experts who will design and develop such law. The initial attempt will be to employ or engage those experts who are within the state's control and will comply with its wishes. Usually, these will be those who are not qualified, or if they are qualified in terms of paper qualifications, they are those who have bartered away their abilities for worldly gains. This will alienate a large body of the experts in the country some of whom are really qualified and who often have a considerable following.

Even when the ulama', as these experts are called, are qualified in the traditional Islamic law, they lack the knowledge of modern institutions, instruments and transactions on the basis of which modern law operates. This is exactly what we mean by growth of Islamic law. It should be able to employ the fundamental principles of Islamic law, analyse modern laws, be able to absorb or Islamize them, or reject them and suggest substitute laws. This means a thorough knowledge of modern laws and modern practices. The ulama, unfortunately, have been kept isolated for centuries first by confining them to their *madaris,* and then by introducing a subject of "Islamic studies," which implies that Islam is merely a "personal affair." All laws developed for the state, even by the leading experts, are subject to suspicion in the sense of being subservient to the goals of the state and not those of Islamic law.

As compared to the state, the law developed by groups that have their own axe to grind, or their own goals to promote, present a somewhat different problem. Their goals are driven by greed and the profit-motive and they succumb to the needs of the market, just like a state may succumb to political pressure. The foremost example here is that of so-called Islamic banks and financial institutions. They hire some ulama', give them huge benefits, and then get the opinions they want. Stories abound as to how these institutions are using the services of experts for their own goals. The phrase "rent a sheikh" has gainned considerable currency.

Even when an atmosphere of impartiality is created in this process, like the creation of standard setting institutions, it is the same experts who are serving the banks who are hired and they ensure that the interests of their parent institutions are secured. The income source of these institutions is dependent upon the Islamic banks, as is the sale of their products. We may cite the case of the State Bank of Pakistan. The qualification fixed for an expert is "Dars Nizami." This certificate is barely equal to the US High school or equal to matriculation in Pakistan. What is the purpose of this qualification? It is obvious that such a person will not know anything about Islamic law either, besides some acts of worship and probably something about marriage and divorce. As for the complex banking transactions or those of commercial law and negotiable instruments, the person will have no knowledge. He will be more than happy to issue the desired rulings.

It is obvious that we cannot expect our ulama' to act like the earlier Imams and jurists. In the early days, some of the leading Imams were brutalized and persecuted. Others like Imām al-Sarakhsī were locked away in prisons. He refused to issue a ruling in favour of the ruler and was kept in prison for 15 years where he produced his major works. They bore these pressures with patience and did not yield for they wanted to maintain the independence and impartiality of Islamic law. It is this independence of the law that was precious for them; it is this spirit that should be precious today: the independnece and freedom of the law. The schools did not serve particular goverments or rulers, they made law that would be applicable uniformly all over the Muslim world.

If it is assumed that the state may at times be directed by people who are sincere and truly wish to serve Islamic law and develop it, then the ulama' should have no objection to cooperating with the state under these cirumstances. This may be true, but the law will be state specific; it will not have that kind of universality that is expected from a school made law that is serving the entire Muslim world. Another problem in this case will be that the state will permit the development of only that part of the law that it needs and not the other essential parts that are needed to complete the law. The overall, systematic and comprehensive development of the law requires that it be developed in a free environment without the intervening needs of vested interests.

3.2 The Meaning of Emergence of the Law at the International Level

We have stated in what has preceded that the declarations, conventions and protocols issued by the United Nations have not adopted a single principle or rule of Islamic law.[42] The

---

[42]The term "declaration" is used for various international instruments. International human rights declarations are not legally binding; the term is often deliberately chosen to indicate that the parties do not intend to create binding obligations but merely want to declare certain aspirations. However, while the 1948 Universal Declaration of Human Rights for example was not originally intended to have binding force, its provisions have since gained binding character as customary law. A "convention" is a formal agreement between States. The generic term "convention" is thus synonymous with the generic term "treaty." Conventions are normally open for participation by the international community as a whole, or by a large number of States. Usually the instruments negotiated under the auspices of an international organization are entitled conventions (e.g. the Convention on the Rights of the Child, adopted by the General Assembly of the United Nations in 1989). The term "protocol" is used for an additional legal instrument that

principles of Islamic law are also not acknowledged in the other sources of international law listed in Article 38 of the Statute for the Permanent Court of International Justice.[43] These other sources are "international custom," "principles" and "judicial decisions and teachings." All these revolve around the Anglo-European-American systems and "civilization." Whenever Muslim countries try to make a "reservation" on the basis of Islamic law, the other states, following the procedure at the UN say that you cannot rely on domestic law for making reservations. In simple words, it means if you wish to raise such objections just stay out. Thus, for example, Muslim states raised some objections to the CRC saying, among other things, that adoption was not allowed in Islam. They were forced to back down and as eyewash a rule for fosterage called *kafalah* in Egyptian law was referred to without having any bearing on the CRC. The rule for *kafalal* is not applied this way in Islamic law, that is, as it is applied in Egyptian law. The crux of the matter is that the structure of binding and non-binding sources of international law, as erected by the UN, is designed to keep out Islamic law, because that is the only logal tradition besides civil law and common law.

---

complements and adds to a treaty. A protocol may be on any topic relevant to the original treaty and is used either to further address something in the original treaty, address a new or emerging concern, or add a procedure for the operation and enforcement of the treaty— such as adding an individual complaints procedure. A protocol is "optional" because it is not automatically binding on States that have already ratified the original treaty; States must independently ratify or accede to a protocol. The Optional Protocols to the Convention on the Rights of the Child concern the involvement of children in armed conflict and the sale of children, child prostitution and child pornography. Theses paragraphs have been transmitted verbatim from the UN Treaty Reference Guide.

[43] Available at http://www.worldcourts.com/pcij/eng/documents/1920.12 16_statute.htm

We also stated that international law exists for facilitating trade in a peaceful manner and for sharing the resources of Earth with justice. One main purpose is the security of international transactions. This goal is so important that if business people find the rules set by nation states or by the United Nations to be too restrictive, they can brush aside those rules and follow the rules that they agree on. When a dispute arises out of their chosen rules, they usually provide that the matter will be taken to arbitration in tribunals of their choice. It is only as a last resort that the matter may be taken to domestic tribunals for enforcement where it will be settled according to the rules of private international law. There are some other matters too where domestic institutions come into play like the carriage of goods and payment systems.

It is generally acknowledged that one of the most remarkable developments on the contemporary legal scene is the emergence of an AUTONOMOUS LAW of private international trade, which is breaking through the barriers of national legal systems and is assuming a universal character. This autonomous body of law provides more effective solutions to the problems of international trade. The result is that it is increasingly replacing the conflict-of-laws approach that applies one of the many national systems of law, when this municipal or national system may be inadequate in the changed circumstances of modern international trade. The success of this autonomous body of law depends upon two things.

1. The first is the elective character of the law. The elective nature of the Law of International Trade exists because this branch of law is founded on the principle of the autonomy of the parties' wills. Such relative freedom in tailoring contracts enables the parties to overcome the peculiarities of the various municipal systems of law, and to adopt rules more suitable to the requirements of their individual relationship. This new, autonomous law is being expressed in model contracts, standard clauses, general terms of delivery, commercial customs and trade

usages. Most of the model contracts are being issued by the International Chamber of Commerce (ICC), which also issues the language that traders speak to make contracts, called INCOTERMS.

2. The second is the effective support, and the growing use, of arbitration in trade disputes. Experience has shown, however, that for the autonomous will of the party to a contract to be considered effective, it has to be complemented by an arbitration agreement. Parties willing to develop rules to govern their relationship apart from municipal laws do not wish to find themselves subject to municipal courts when disputes arise. They prefer arbitral tribunals where customs, usages, and business practices are more readily taken into account.

The principles of this autonomous law have been issued by UNIDROIT, which is an institute that came into existence at the time of the League of Nations, but is not a UN body. These principles are gradually gaining ground. The UN body that is occupied with a similar task of creating uniform commercial law is called the UNCITRAL, which has issued the convention on the sale of goods, called the CISG, but that is a UN binding document. It has been ratified by more than 60 states so far and is gaining more ground in Europe.

Our purpose here is only to indicate the existence of an autonomous law at the international level, which is a law that individual concerns may choose for themselves and support with a system of arbitration. The main purpose of this discussion is to show that ISLAMIC LAW HAS BEEN AN AUTONOMOUS LAW FUNCTIONING AT THE INTERNATIONAL LEVEL SINCE ITS BIRTH. As indicated earlier, the *qāḍīs* operated more like arbitration tribunals. It was only where the schools of law had imposed a duty upon the rulers that the public law was applied by these judges. The rulers too were free to choose the school that they liked for this purpose, that is, for the adopting the rules for *ḥudūd* and *qiṣāṣ*, for example.

What we mean by the emergence of Islamic law at the international level as an autonomous law is the following:

1. Islamic law must grow at the international level as an autonomous law free from the constraints and needs of modern states.

2. It should develop and grow with the aim of providing solutions to modern issues and problems.

3. Islamic law should develop in a manner that it can be adopted and adapted by states if they so wish.

4. Islamic law should grow, at the international level, in all those areas that can employ arbitral tribunals for the resolution of problems.

5. Islamic law should grow at the international level with the active participation of those who are interested in its development and who wish to contribute to its growth.

6. In its development and growth, the law should employ the uniform and latest methodology that was developed by the ancestors.

7. Islamic law must grow into a uniform law acceptable to all Muslims, at least in areas where that is possible, leaving other areas to be followed according to the various schools that individuals choose for themselves.

What is of crucial significance is that the law must develop free of all school bias. Further, this law must not focus on personalities, unless these are the earlier Imams, preferably those of the sixth century Hijrah and earlier. The entire focus should be on what the rule is and what is the evidence on which it is based along with the accompanying legal reasoning.

3.3   The Way the Proposed Emergence Can Commence

We may briefly list a few important areas that belong to the core law of Islam that contains measures that are likely to provide substantial benefit to Muslims all over the world. The priorities may, however, be changed if the Muslims so decide.

3.3.1   *Zakāt* and *Ṣadqaqāt*

The Law of *zakāt* should be developed from the international perspective as a global system in the service of the Muslim Ummah. The law of *ṣadaqāt* (voluntary charity) should also be developed for the help of mankind in general.

Some of the major questions to be asked must be whether *zakāt* collected can be moved across the entire expanse of earth to fight hunger and poverty in the Muslim world. It should also be explored as to what kind of financial or other institution will perform the function of distribution of *zakāt* as well as *ṣadaqāt*. Institutions trying to perform these functions already must show that they are performing functions according to an acceptable uniform *zakāt* law. These institutions should also make their affairs more transparent.

3.3.2   *Ḥajj* and *'Umrā*

The rules of *ḥajj* and *'umrā* should be refined and expanded in the light of modern issues faced by worshippers. Other issues from the other acts of worship may also be included, especially those related to timings and so on.

3.3.3   Developments in the Medical Field and the Ruling of Islamic Law

Scholars of Islamic law keep on addressing modern developments in the field of medicine, however, this entire research needs to be restated in the form of a law. The most important developments may be taken up first.

3.3.4   Modern methods of food creation and distribution

This is a crucial area that needs immediate attention, especially in the light of the growth and use of genetically modified foods. The rules must lay down the requirements for the food industry, halal food and so on. Medicines and drugs using prohibited matter may be included in this area. These matters should not be left to the countries where the relevant industries are based.

3.3.5   Rules and Recommendations for Countries Where Discrimination Against Muslims May Exist

The discrimination contemplated here is based on clothing, acts of worship and religious practices, religious education or the other preferences of the concerned nations. Genocide of Muslims may also be included under this head if deemed necessary. Most of these issues will arise where Muslims are in a minority.

3.3.6   Islamic Commercial Law and Arbitration

This is perhaps the most important area. Initially, the UNIDROIT principles and the CISG will first be analysed from the Islamic perspective so as to find common ground with the rest of the world. In other words, an attempt will be made to Islamize these principles so that the United Nations realizes the requirements of Muslims living in this world and who will be rapidly moving towards a majority mark in world population.

The mechanism for setting up and implementing arbitration tribunals will also be explored.

Efforts will also be needed to analyze the payment systems so as to identify the changes that may be needed from the Islamic perspective. To this may be added the needs of banking and finance, if deemed necessary, as the mechanism set up will provide an unbiased and impartial analysis.

3.3.7   Family Law and Associated Tribunals

Matters of family law will be studied to develop a uniform law that can be followed by Muslims all over the world. Tribunals may be set up for meeting the dispute resolution needs of this vital area.

3.3.8   Looking Into the Future

Gradually, Islamic law must step into every area that is being addressed by the United Nations, and give its ruling and analysis. Thus, for example, it can start by issuing the Islamic Declaration of Human Rights or even begin examining the Human Rights Declaration to see what needs to be changed. In either case, the effort must identify the principles that need to be recognized by the United Nations. If the current human rights are claimed to be universal and indivisible, they must incorporate Islamic principles. It may be pointed out here that Islamic principles are equally universal and indivisible. The declaration may or may not rely on the Cairo Declaration.

Declarations should be issued whenever and wherever it is felt that the United Nations is ignoring certain fundamental principles of Islamic law. Declarations will be needed for the political and economic rights as well as on the rights of women and children.

The following organisations and institutions may be contemplated for future action:

- International Zakat and Sadaqat Organization

- Islamic Court of International Arbitration

- International Institute for Uniform Islamic Commercial Law

- Islamic Trade Organisation

- Islamic Food and Drug Organisation

- Islamic Labour Organisation for Migrant Populations

- International Islamic Criminal Court

- Islamic Human Rights Organisation

- Islamic Financial Organisation

It is suggested that Universities in the Muslim World, especially those departments that deal with law and international relations should encourage research in the above areas. There has been too much occpation with armed conflict and international humanitarian law; students must open their minds to other vital areas to see where the Muslims of the world stand on such issues.

3.4   Resolving and Accommodating the Differences Between the Schools of Law

The first question that will come to mind for most is about the multiple opinions on an issue within a school, and many more when the scope is expanded to include other schools. What then will the people follow? The response is that as the law is not being enforced through the state and its enforcement mechanism, much depends on what the people will choose for themselves.

In the case of acts of worship (*ibādāt*), people will follow the school they are following now. Any new issue taken up will be one that the school has not addressed. In such a case, following the rule in the new issue should not be a problem. For example, many new issues pertaining to purification, prayers, fasting, *ḥajj* and so on have already been addressed, even those that have arisen in the modern times. In the case of *zakāt*, the amount to be paid and other details may be the same as those addressed by the schools. The new issues will pertain to the collection and distribution from the international level and the possibility of permitting this.

In the case of marriage and divorce, people will continue to follow what the schools have said. Many new issues arising due to the domicile and school of the parties to a marriage contract are not new issues and have already been addressed by the schools. As for the new issues in this area, these will be those that have not been addressed by the schools, and will have no ruling within individual schools. It will be easy to follow the new rulings on new issues.

As far as international commercial law is concerned, it is only some fundamental principles that are of vital significance. There is not much difference among the schools between these fundamentals. The details developed by the jurists will be given new shape in any case in accordance with the needs of modern commerce, trade and financial transactions.

The bulk of the law will have to be developed in the light of the fundamentals of Islamic law according to the new methodology that is to be introduced in the next chapter. These will be issues on which there is no ruling in the schools.

The above description shows that there is no serious issue about differing views of jurists and schools. The law at the international level will be much more flexible and vibrant as will be explained in the following two chapters.

CHAPTER 4

MEETING THE NEED FOR A UNIVERSAL METHODOLOGY OR UNIVERSAL *UṢŪL AL-FIQH*

The new methodology, following what al-Shāṭibī said, does not need a knowledge of Arabic. Arabic, however, will be an additional asset for the new methodology. Any language may be used. For purposes of this document, we are assuming that English will be used.

It is obvious that a thorough acquaintance with Islamic jurisprudence is necessary. Any book on Islamic jurisprudence (*uṣūl al-Fiqh*), written in any language, may be used for the purpose. This does not apply to *fiqh* however. Some knowledge of *fiqh*, acquired from a manual of *fiqh* of any school, will be a prerequisite. Thus, for the Ḥanafī school, the *Hidāyah* may be used, however, any earlier manual will serve the purpose. Modern texts, whatever their popularity, are no substitute for an earlier work.

A short book will soon be written that will explain the new methodology through examples, so that those interested in contributing may be able to adopt the new methodology with ease. The new methodology, however, is not one that has been developed by the present writer or by any other modern writer. It was a methodology developed by the earlier jurists after they had completed the task of interpreting the texts of the Qur'ān and the Sunnah. They crafted the new methodology for the issues they had not addressed themselves. The methodology was meant to address new issues in every new age, but not to demolish the earlier work carried out by the jurists. The main requirement of the new methodology is that the new rulings issued must somehow incorporate, or be based upon, the norms of the *sharī'ah*.

Those who have read our earlier works will recognize at once what we are talking about.

In what follows in this chapter, we will highlight three major features of this new methodology. These features will not explain the details of the methodology and how it is to be implemented, something that will be done in a small book that will follow soon, but they will act as a pointer to the path that is to be taken. Two of these features are not new, and we have already discussed them in our earlier works. Accordingly, we will reproduce what we said in those earlier texts.

4.1   The Two Spheres of Islamic Law

The first feature was explained in our book entitled *Theories of Islamic law* (1994). This feature was that Islamic law operates within two related spheres, one fixed and the other flexible. We will reproduce that text with slight modifications where necessary.[44]

[Quote Begins] Islamic law is like an ever-growing tree. The seed of this tree was sown in the hearts and minds of men, fourteen hundred years ago, by Muḥammad, the Messenger of Allāh (pbuh). Since then it has taken root, grown, and spread its branches on all sides. With each passing century, the tree grows in size. Its evolution and growth never stop. Its spreading branches cast their shade on all sides covering different cultures, peoples, and races.

Like the trunk of this tree, Islamic law has a part that is fixed, and like its branches and leaves, the law has a part that changes in shape and color in every season. The fixed part of this tree is closer to the roots and cutting this part is likely to damage the tree itself. Like the trunk of this tree, the fixed part of Islamic law has grown directly from its roots or sources. Changing this fixed part

---

[44]The text is excerpted from the author's *Theories of Islamic Law*.

will affect the nature of the legal system. Like the branches of the tree, the flexible part of the law has been changing with the times, sometimes yielding abundant fruit, sometimes less.

When the branches of this tree are cut off, its cool shade is missing, but its strong trunk continues to guide and protect those who cling to it in storms and times of crisis. Thus, when the "state" does not let the branches of Islamic law provide their shade, it is the fixed part that continues to keep the Muslims on the right track. For those Muslims living in secular states, the fixed part of the tree is the only guide, and this is all they are obliged to follow, except for certain parts that are beyond their power to implement.

Tending the trunk of the tree, the fixed part, has always been the task of Muslim jurists (the *fuqahā'*). They have looked after it with loving care for fourteen centuries. Their labour has made the trunk so strong that ceaseless attacks against it have failed to budge it. Not only this, many attacks on its roots have also failed. When the tree was young, its stem was tended jointly by the "state" and the jurists, as then there was no distinction between the fixed and the flexible part. It was later, when the tree reached a mature stage of development, that the fixed part could be distinguished from the changing part with ease. At this stage the jurists left the care of the flexible part in the hands of the *imām* or the state, while they devoted themselves to the strengthening and refinement of the fixed part of the law. The only condition that the jurists imposed upon the *imām* for developing the flexible part of the law was that he be a qualified jurist (*mujtahid*), that is, he should employ a valid methodology, either directly or through delegation, for developing this part of the law.

The rulers in some ages did care for the branches of this tree, while in others they did not. On occasions, some rulers cut off the branches that had grown in earlier ages and started all over again. This discouraged the development of firm offshoots from the tree, that is, the development of legal institutions and practices that

Figure 4.1:   The Growing Tree

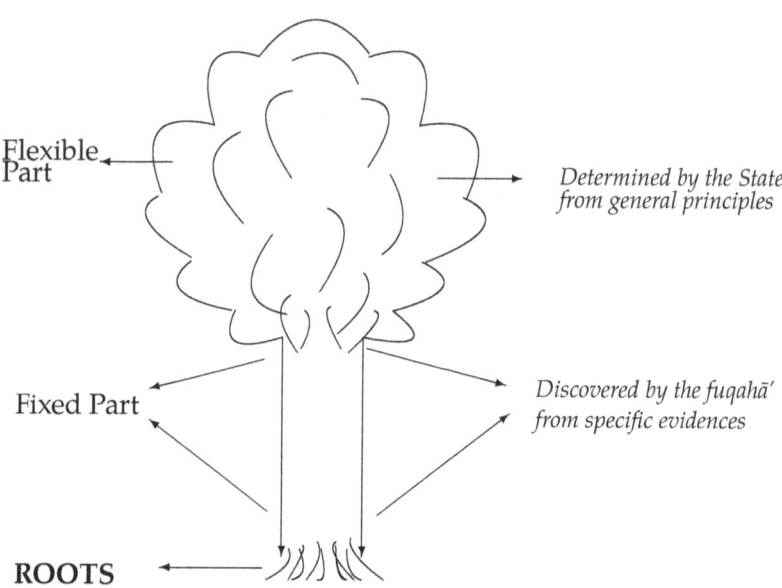

Flexible Part   *Determined by the State from general principles*

Fixed Part   *Discovered by the fuqahā' from specific evidences*

ROOTS

could be developed further in later ages. After some centuries, when the Muslim empire split up, the branches of the tree were divided into different segments on different sides, with each ruler looking after the branches on his own side of the tree, as it suited his wisdom. Some took interest in this law while others did not. Thus, for example, the Ottoman rulers tended these branches in their own way in the Ottoman empire, while Awrangzeb 'Ālamgīr developed the law in his own fashion in India.

The period of these rulers was followed by violent storms around this tree, and alien winds struck it destroying the branches on all sides. On some sides the Muslims pulled down the branches themselves. The age of colonization left nothing, but the solid trunk of the tree, which could not be uprooted with ease, thanks to centuries of dedicated work by Muslim jurists. When the storms were over and the Muslims were left alone to take care of the tree, all they could see was the trunk of the tree with no branches or leaves. In their confusion they started blaming the jurists for not having looked after the branches, and having fallen prey to *taqlīd*. They failed to distinguish between the fixed part and the flexible part. They did not realize that it was some of the rulers and not the jurists who were to blame for not having established lasting institutions. Some even tried to bring branches from other alien trees to hang on their own tree, least realizing that these would rot one day. Today, some Muslim states are trying to look after the tree in their own way and on their own side, while others are busy trying to cut down the tree and even dig at its very roots. Nevertheless, branches have begun to sprout and it will not be too long before they start to bear fruit. Indeed, they must bear fruit, because the culture, history, life, and the very identity of Muslims are associated with this tree.

The word evolution when used with Islamic law is likely to evoke different reactions. Those who feel that the *sharī'ah* was laid down once and for all may reject the idea of evolution in Islamic law. Their objections are partly justified. But, as Islamic law is meant to apply to every aspect of a Muslim's life in all ages, it follows that it has to evolve and grow like any other legal system so that it may be able to cater to the demands of the changing times. This is exactly what it does and is designed to do. The *sharī'ah* may be fixed and immutable at its central core, as is claimed by some,[45] but is not so in its extensions. The truth is that Islamic law grew gradually to become a complete legal system. The nature of its growth resembles that of a seed embedded in fertile soil. The seed contained within it the genetic code of the entire legal system. It grew into a living organism that would constantly adapt itself to the changes in its environment. The laws in the Qur'ān and the *Sunnah* of the Prophet (pbuh), it is true, have been determined and fixed for all times to come. These comprise the core legal concepts,

---

[45]See Noel J. Coulson, "The State and the Individual in Islamic Law," *The International and the Comparative Law Quarterly*, 6 (1957): 49–60.

the genetic code, so to say. As Muḥammad (pbuh) was the last of the prophets, there is no chance of mutation in these laws. Calls for *ijtihād* in the present age, if they are meant to alter such fixed laws, are futile and unnecessary. These fixed laws, however, cover a relatively small area of the activity of a modern state, and the bulk of the laws remain to be discovered. The system continues to grow. [Quote Ends]

The above text, reproduced from the text mentioned, explains one aspect of the nature of the Islamic system. For further details, the said book may be consulted.

4.2 No Need to Reinvent the Wheel for the Interpretation of the Texts

In the previous section, we have said that Islamic law has a fixed unalterable part and a flexible maleable part that is waiting to grow. The occupation of modern writers, thinkers and jurists has been with the fixed part. They have been trying their best to undo the fixed part, at least those rules of it that are offensive to the West. To understand the methods of modern scholars, the task undertaken by the earlier jurists has to be appreciated in broad terms.

Ijtihād means interpretation of the legal texts of the Qur'ān and the Sunnah. It does not mean deriving rulings from the general principles of natural law or some other system and then passing off your views as being part of the *sharī'ah* or Islamic law. *Ijtihād* can never be outside the legal texts of the Qur'ān and the Sunnah. Consequently, the earlier jurists never moved out of the ambit of these texts. It was these jurists who were the authorities for the interpretation of the legal texts of the Qur'an and the Sunnah, whichever school they belonged to. The writers of *tafsīrs* of the Qur'ān are not the authority for the interpretation of these legal texts, unless they are jurists too, which was the case on many occasions.

The point to be made here is that these authorities, over the centuries, have considered and listed almost all possible meanings that could be derived from the legal texts. All the verses from which legal meanings could be derived were so derived by the jurists and stated in their manuals or in works called *aḥkām al-Qur'ān*. The meanings included those that could be derived directly or by implication and syllogistic extensions. The jurists also derived all kinds of underlying causes or *'ilal* for use in different types of analogy. These were tallied with the general principles arising from the legal texts, either directly or through derivation. This was done through a process called *istiḥsān*, as well as through certain types of *maṣlaḥah* (extended analogy). To quote al-Shawkānī, for example, for the texts dealing with *ribā* the jurists derived nineteen underlying causes.

The result of this sincere, dedicated and prolonged activity spreading over centuries was that very little room was left for new views on these legal texts or for deriving new rules from them beyond what the earlier jurists had done. It is true that an occasional interpretation in a new way might be possible, but this was rare and exceptional. Modern scholars then felt cramped for room. What they started doing was to list a large number of different opinions and then saying, "This is what we choose," or "This is what we pick." The problem was, or still is, that this picking and choosing has no system, no declared or undeclared methodology. It is like the act of a person who aranges flowers of different colours before him, then closes his eyes and puts his finger on one saying, "This is what I choose." It amounts to blind, misguided and whimsical *taqlīd*, which is to be condemned outright.

The problem, however, is that if the jurists have done all the work of interpretation of the legal texts, leaving very little room or opportunity for further interpretation, then what is a modern jurist to do? How is he to go about solving modern problems on the basis of the legal texts? The answer given by the jurists was simple. Instead of using indidiual texts for issues, they said, use all the texts together. This meant, use the purposes of the *sharī'ah* or the *maqāṣid al-sharī'ah*.

Modern scholars tried to use the puposes of law, but in their enthusiasm they forgot the details and the conditions associated with these purposes. They used them in a haphazard manner, thus, losing sight of what was required. Many of them just mentioned the *maqāṣid* and then proceeded to use their own reason, based on natural law or something else, to arrive at the ruling of their choice. This approach creates more suspicion rather than confidence.

The jurists, when they proposed the use of the texts all at once or the use of the purposes, they also laid down the method through which these purposes were to be used. In addition to this, they also showed how the whole methodology is to be linked with the discipline of *uṣūl al-fiqh*. The details of this methodology will be provided in a small book to be written, and which has already been mentioned above. For the present we may just mention what is meant by the purposes of the *sharī'ah*.

Before we talk about the rationale of the new methodology, it is essential to point out the significance of the series called "Laws of the Qur'ān and the Sunnah." We have stated that the jurists continued to interpret the texts of the Qur'ān and the Sunnah for centuries. In addition to this, they derived numerous underlying causes from the texts. This series will present an authentic record of this monumental work of the jurists. Not only will it present the record of these interpretations, it will also attempt to indicate the areas where the possibility exists for further interpretation. A major area of focus will be the principles and rules around which the entire edifice of Islamic law has been erected; these rules and principles will be highlighted as they will play a major role in the proposed new methodology. Another task that this series may perform is to correct the distortions that have been brought into the law in the modern times, especially by bodies working for business or financial interests, or even those that are biased towards a particular brand of ideology and are pushing the agenda of that methodology. This, however, should not mean that the work of these bodies is to be examined with some kind of bias. All good things must be willingly accepted. The series will, therefore, act as an ideal source for learning Islamic law and then participating in the efforts contemplated under Lex Islamica in the previous sections.

4.3 The Rationale of the New Methodology

We have mentioned, and talked about, the *maqāṣid* in different works. The last work in which they were explained briefly was our book entitled *Islamic Legal Maxims* (2013). The text given below is reproduced from this book.

4.3.1 *Siyāsah Shar'iyyah*: The Legal and Social Policies of the *Sharī'ah*

[Quote Begins] Herbert Broom begins his famous book on legal maxims with the the maxims falling under "Rules Founded on Public Policy." The first maxim he discusses is *Salus Populi suprema Lex* or "Public welfare is the supreme law." The maxim really means that indivdual interest will be given up in the face of public interest or necessity. Thus, the law may even ask the individual to give up his property, or even life, for the public welfare or interest. The second maxim is about a private inividual acting under necessity, and is similar to the maxim "necessity knows no law."[46] It should be stated at the outset that *maṣlaḥah* and *maqāṣid al-sharī'ah* in Islamic law play a much wider role: it is not public interest alone that is being addressed and the underlying ideas are

---

[46]The other maxims considered under this head are: That rule of conduct is to be deemed binding which religion dictates; and Sunday is not a day for judicial or legal proceedings.

quite different from the Western idea of pubic interest discussed in these maxims. The maxim about welfare above does have a parallel in Islamic law too:

$$\text{تَصَرُّفُ الْإِمَامِ عَلَى الرَّعِيَّةِ مَنُوطٌ بِالْمَصْلَحَةِ}$$

The actions of the Imam affecting the subjects are based on *maṣlaḥah* (human interests or welfare)

The main distinction is that the idea of public and private interests in Islamic law has been ordained by the Lawgiver, Allah Almighty, while public interest in law has been determined by the human mind with all its limitations.

It is not our purpose in this chapter to describe the *maqāṣid al-sharī'ah* or even *siyāsah shar'iyyah* in detail. We have already done this in our books called *Theories of Islamic law* and *Islamic jurisprudence*. We will only record here what is relevant to the present discussion and the legal concept involved. Let us begin with the basic terms to be used in this chapter, so that the reader does not have a problem understanding them.

4.3.2   The Basic Terms of This Topic

The *maqāṣid al-sharī'ah* are the five ultimate principles that the *sharī'ah* places before us as objectives or goals to be achieved. The word *qaṣd* is also translated literally as intention, and in this sense these five principles reflect the intention of the Lawgiver. Both meanings will be used in this chapter, in different contexts, and the meaning will become clear. The five principles are:

- *Dīn* (the system) has to be preserved and protected.

- *Nafs* (life) has to be preserved and protected.

- *Nasl* (progeny or the family system) has to be preserved and protected.

- *'Aql* (intellect or reason) has to be preserved and protected.

- *Māl* (property and wealth) has to be preserved and protected.

"Preserved and protected" are two words indicating a similar meaning, but the jurists have indicated to us that these reflect two different faces of these principles. By preserved we mean to affirm, to develop, and to make the system contained in the principle to grow to its full maturity and potential. By protection we mean the defence of what has been developed. This is done by defending against invasions and by providing penalties and remedies for infringements and violations.

The term *siyāsah shar'iyyah* (سياسة شرعيّة) means the policy of the *sharī'ah*. The policy is just as long as the government (note that we do not use the alien concept of state) upholds the *sharī'ah*. If it does not uphold it, the policy becomes unjust or *zālimah*. The policy of the *sharī'ah* is of two types: the first deals with the "preservation" aspect of the five principles listed above, while the second deals with the "protection" aspect of these five principles.

The policy dealing with the "preservation" aspect we will call the "social policy of the *sharī'ah*." This policy identifies the goals to be attained by the system or the targets to be achieved by the *imām* or government. The duties of the government are contained in this policy. This public policy is relevant for the legislature and the executive, and they are duty bound to uphold and implement this policy. Economists should focus on this aspect, while the legislators should convert what is deemed immediate into law or legislation. The executive must base its proposals and policies on this aspect, and seek to implement it as far as possible.

The policy dealing with the "protection" aspect we will call the "legal policy of the *sharī'ah*." It consists of all the principles, presumptions (whether legislative or other), *dawābit* and targets meant for the judicial system. It is similar to what the Germans have called *rechtspolitik*. This is the domain of the jurist, the judge and the lawyer; they must always uphold them during adjudication and elaboration. It is to be noted that principles and rules contain "rights" and thus the *bāb* of rights becomes directly relevant here.

It may be pointed out here that Ronald Dworkin has drawn fine distinctions between policy and principle, and the reader may refer to his works. Nevertheless, our use of the terms social policy and legal policy may be slightly different from the way he has used these terms.

The legal policy of the common law has taken centuries to develop through the effort of the judges and lawyers. Islamic law is no different. It took the jurists centuries to refine these policies by going over the texts in minute detail and by issuing rulings spread over centuries. The difference between Islamic law and common law is that the social and legal policies of the *sharī'ah* were refined and fully developed long before common law was even born. And who knows the common law may even have borrowed much from Islamic law: as some say the word *assissez* of the common law is nothing more than a translation of the word *siyāsah*.

In our earlier works, we have traced the development of the *maqāṣid al-sharī'ah* at length. Here we would like to record a few more facts that shed light on this development. This will be instructive for those who wish to take up research in this area. The next few paragraphs are, therefore, devoted to the growth of the policies reflected in the five principles. After doing so, we will describe the two policies briefly.

4.3.3   The Development of the Five Principles and Area of Operation

In our book *Theories of Islamic Law* (published 1994), we had stated that the initial ideas about *maqāṣid al-sharī'ah* were generated by al-Juwaynī and then it was al-Ghazālī who developed a fully fledged theory about the purposes of Islamic law. The fact, however, is that the ideas are much older. Some people continue to believe, incorrectly, that the ideas originated with al-Shāṭibī, who lived centuries after al-Ghazālī. We will talk about al-Shāṭibī's contribution in the next section. The reason why it is important to discover the origin of the ideas about this field is to show that it took centuries to refine the ideas. In addition to this, talking about the origin of the ideas may also indicate the purpose for which these ideas were developed, thus telling us how the *maqāṣid* are to be used.

The origin of the ideas appears first in the work of al-Dabbūsī. The ideas are scattered in his work and are not presented in the form of a coherent theory. It is possible that the discussion found in his work might have taken place even earlier. We have already pointed out that al-Dabbūsī has had a very deep impact on the development of *uṣūl al-fiqh* and on the writings of later jurists, even those belonging to other schools, like al-Juwaynī and al-Ghazālī. Al-Dabbūsī first discusses the objective of the causes that make the *aḥkām* obligatory. These causes are imposed by the Lawgiver and the subject has no role in the creation of the obligation. After discussing these purposes in several places, he says the following:

> This is based on the argument that Allah, the Exalted, has not prohibited anything out of the things available except on the basis of interests (*maṣāliḥ*) that (ultimately) revert to us through the prohibition. Thus, He has prohibited *zinā* (unlawful sexual intercourse) insofar as there is the ruination of progeny in it due to the absence of rearing. He has prohibited excess in consumption insofar as there is wastage in it. He has prohibited *khamr* (wine) insofar as it leads to deficiency of intellect, prevention from the remembrance of Allah, and behaviour like that of a madman. He has prohibited gambling insofar as there is hatred and enmity in it as well as the destruction of wealth ....

Al-Dabbūsī's most devoted follower, in *uṣūl* as well as *fiqh*, Shams al-A'immah al-Sarakhsī had the following to say after about forty years:

يقرره ان تبديل الدين وأصل الكفر من أعظم الجنايات ولكنها بين العبد وبين ربه فالجزاء عليها مؤخر الي دار الجزاء وما عجل في الدنيا سياسات مشروعة لمصالح تعود إلى العباد كالقصاص لصيانة النفوس وحد الزنا لصيانة الانساب والفرش وحد السرقة لصيانة الاموال وحد القذف لصيانة الاعراض وحد الخمر لصيانة العقول

This is affirmed by the fact that changing one's religion and original unbelief are the greatest of all offences, but this is something between the slave and his Creator. Consequently, the recompense is deferred till (reaching) the House of Recompense (the Hereafter). What has been hastened in this world are the legal policies for securing interests that (ultimately) revert to the servants, like *qiṣāṣ* for the protection of lives, the *ḥadd* of *zinā* for the protection of progeny and family (for rearing), the *ḥadd* of *sariqah* for the protection of property/wealth, the *ḥadd* of *qadhf* for the protection of reputations, and the *ḥadd* of *khamr* for the protection of intellects.

This is explicit and it shows that the discussions about the *maqāṣid* must have reached an advanced stage before al-Ghazālī took over. The most important point in this passage is that the *maqāṣid* are called "legal policies" (*siyāsāt mashrū'ah*) by al-Sarakhsī. This limits the role of the *maqāṣid* to *siyāsah shar'iyyah*. Al-Juwaynī also indicated that these interests are to be used within *siyāsah*.

The net result is that the *maqāṣid al-sharī'ah* cannot be used to overturn the law that has been derived directly from the texts or through methods like *qiyās*. The *maqāṣid* are to be used for new issues and for solving new legal or social problems.

4.3.4   The Content of the Policies

The content of these policies has been described by us in our other works under the heading of "the two faces of the *maqāṣid*." What was said there is briefly reproduced here with slight amendments.

Perhaps the most important feature of the *maqāṣid* is their dual thrust. Al-Ghazālī discusses this dual nature in detail in his book called *Jawāhir al-Qur'ān*.[47] This point has been ignored by almost all the later jurists, except for al-Shāṭibī.

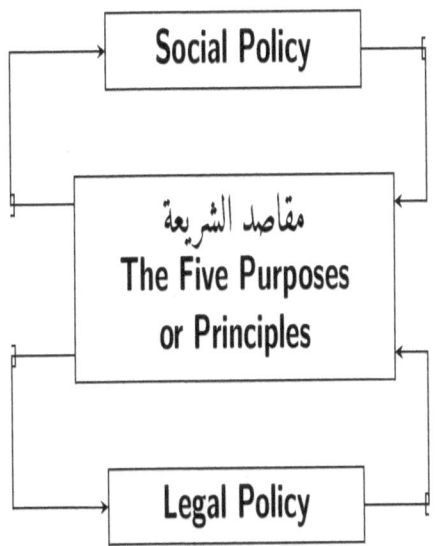

Social Policy

مقاصد الشريعة
The Five Purposes
or Principles

Legal Policy

The dual feature of the *maqāṣid* is evident in the use of the terms *ibqā'* and *ḥifẓ*, which we may call preservation and protection. Al-Shāṭibī considers these the two aspects of *ḥifẓ*. The first he says is "what affirms its elements and establishes its foundations."[48]

---

[47] Al-Ghazālī, *Jawāhir al-Qur'ān* (Beirut: Dār Ihyā' al-'Ulūm, 1985), 32-35

[48] Al-Shāṭibī, *al-Muwafaqāt*, vol. 2, 8.

The second is "what repels actual or expected disharmony."[49] The focus of later jurists, and hence that of modern scholars, has been on the aspect of protection alone. Each purpose, however, has a positive or aggressive aspect and a negative or defensive aspect. These are what we have now called the social policy and the legal policy of the *sharī'ah*.

From the positive aspect, or the aspect of social policy, the interest is secured by establishing what is required by the *sharī'ah* through each of its *maqāṣid*. Thus, the interest of *dīn* is secured by the creation of conditions that facilitate worship and establish the other essential pillars of Islam. The interest of life is secured by creating conditions for the existence of life. The interest of progeny is supported by facilitating and establishing family life. The interest of intellect is secured by promoting the means for the growth of the intellect. The interest of wealth is secured by creating proper conditions for the growth of wealth.[50]

From the defensive or the protective aspect, which we have now called the legal policy, interests are secured by preventing the destruction or corruption of the positive aspect. Thus, *jihād* is prescribed for defending *dīn*, while prayer, fasting, pilgrimage, and *zakāh* help establish it. It is the duty of the *imām* to ensure proper conditions for both, while it is binding upon each subject to fulfil these duties, individually and collectively. Life is preserved through the provision of sustenance and the maintenance of good health, while it is protected or defended through the provision of penalties for those who destroy life without legal justification. *Nasl* is promoted through the maintenance of healthy family life and the institution of marriage, while penalties are provided for those who would corrupt it and destroy its values. The preservation of *'aql* is achieved through the provision of education and healthy conditions for its growth, while penalties are provided for the consumption of substances that destroy the

---

[49] Ibid.
[50] Ibid., 2, 9.

intellect. Preservation of wealth is achieved by encouraging its growth, while theft or misappropriation of wealth is punished through penalties.

It is to be noted that al-Sarakhsī has called each separate purpose as a policy. He refers to them collectively as *siyāsāt* or policies. Work needs to be done to work out the details of each policy. We may now turn to how these policies are to be used for creating new law.

4.3.5   Converting Policies into New Law

The law that has been derived by the earlier jurists is not the subject-matter for these policies within the context of alteration and amendment. The policies do explain the earlier law. These policies, however, have a very effective role to play for the creation of new law.

In our book, *Theories of Islamic Law*, we have already explained at length how these policies are to be used for the creation of new law. Here we will say briefly that for every new law that is to be created, the legislator or even the judge, when he is creating a new rule, has to formulate the rule in the form of a proposition. This proposition must conform with the legal policy or the *maqāṣid*; it must not attempt to go against the implication of a legal text; and finally it must be compatible with the general principles of Islamic law, like the general principles discussed in this book. Once the rule clears these benchmarks, the legislator or the judge may go ahead and apply it to the fact situations under consideration. [Quote Ends]

The quoted text ends here. Let us now tie up the whole discussion by repeating what has been said in the last paragraph. The new methodology is to be used in the area of the flexible sphere described above. It cannot be used to overturn things in the fixed sphere, unless an obvious error is detected. As the use of this new methodology is based upon the use of rules and principles, and these are concepts that can be elaborated in any language,

Arabic is not required for the application of this methodology. Further discussion of the new methodology will be undertaken in a separate book.

4.4   The Role of the Specialist

Tthe description of the above methodology may give the impression that anyone with some basic knowledge can use the new methodology. This is true to some extent, but does the specialist, who has devoted a considerable part of his life to the study of *uṣūl* and *fiqh*, have no significant or privileged role in this activity? The rules pertaining to the fixed part have already been settled by the earier jurists and the schools, so what part of the methodology and the law is the modern specialist to deal with? Has all his knowledge attained with so much effort no relevance in all this enterprise?

Nothing could be farther from the truth. The modern expert in *uṣūl* and *fiqh* has a crucial role to play. First, it goes without saying that he will participate like everyone else in the development of new rules by the use of the new methodology in a more effective way. Second, and this perhaps is important, that he will reformulate the rules embedded within *fiqh*. What do we mean by reformulating the rules.

In the previous paragraphs we have said that a person using the new methodology must ensure that his derived rule, which he will employ to settle the issue before him, does "not attempt to go against the implication of a legal text (Qur'ān or Sunnah); and finally it must be compatible with the general principles of Islamic law." The earlier jurists did not express the rules and the priciples in a manner that the modern mind is used to. but the rules are there embedded inside their texts on *fiqh*. The specialist must extract these principles and rules that the person using the new methodology needs for the verification of the rule derived by him. Modern specialists have already done significant work on Islamic law, but the focus has not been on the extraction and reformulation of the rules.

CHAPTER 5

LAUNCHING THE NEW UNIVERSAL METHODOLOGY
FOR THE DEVELOPMENT OF THE LAW

In the previous chapters, it has been outlined at some length as to what areas of Islamic law may be developed at the international level as an "autonomous law" without the constraints or restrictions that are present when it develops within the confines of the state. This law developed in a state of freedom and impartiality may be used voluntarily by individuals all over the world. If found adequate and developed, it may be adopted by Muslim majority states if they choose to do so in matters suitable for them.

5.1   An Invitation to Participate in the Development

The development of the law may be commenced with modest beginnings and later expanded to cover other areas that are being developed by the United Nations. It is obvious that the development of such an autonomous law is not within the capacity of an individual or even a group of dedicated individuals. Nevertheless, a beginning must be made and such a group of persons can be very effective in launching the autonomous law.

The development of this law must not take place under the shadow of personalities, howsoever respected they may be and whatever the number of their followers. Every person, well known or not, should have an opportunity to offer what he wishes to contribute to this noble project. To achieve this, it is essential to focus on the rule or rules proposed, and on the reasoning underlying the rules. Age and gender of the contributor to the project are not to be taken into account when considering the rules proposed.

What is needed is a website where interested persons can discuss and send their contributions and ideas. Those who wish to make a more detailed contribution should have the facility of an online journal to meet the objectives of indepth research. Such a journal may be launched after the proposed website has been launched. The journal will be called "Islamic Law Review," and a major part of its information will be displayed on the website. The contributions made to this journal will be published after peer review and careful selection. The articles published will have the opportunity to influence studies included in "Laws of the Qur'ān and the Sunnah Series" with proper credit given to the authors. The work of the contributors will also help in developing areas of the law included in the "Lex Islamica" project. The Lex Islamica project is to have its own website that will serve as an archiving facility and a forum for those interested in developing the law and exchanging ideas.

5.2   Series on the Laws of the Qur'ān and the Sunnah

To initiate work on the project, a series called "Laws of the Qur'ān and the Sunnah" is also being launched. The content provided through this series may initially serve as basic material upon which others can build. The areas that have been prioritized for this purpose include *zakāt*, family law and commercial law. These areas will be given more pace, although the content will be presented sequentially according to the order of the legal verses in the Qur'ān. Once published, the material will be made available to all for development, refinement and improvement. Articles written with reference to such content will be published in "Islamic Law Review." Articles need not be confined to these topics and contributors will be free to write on any topic that they deem important.

Readers will be encouraged to contribute content according to their own schools, and this will be accommodated. An effort will be made, however, to avoid the tilt toward any particular school, as far as possible. The aim will be to identify the various interpretations assigned by the jurists to the texts and the methods of extension used for expanding such meanings. The series on the "Laws of the Qur'ān and the Sunnah" is being launched with this introduction to Lex Islamica.

The content of the series will deal with the essential material that is necessary according to a legal study of the Qur'ān and the Sunnah, however, for all new issues an attempt will be made to employ the new methodology. In the area of commercial law, the opportunity to employ the new methodology will be greater, which is the major objective of this whole exercise. Employing the new methodology wherever possible will also provide an opportunity to refine this methodology. The effort made in this series will serve as a possible model for those who wish to contribute to the different areas with which the Lex Islamica project is concerned.

BIBLIOGRAPHY

August, Ray. *Public International Law: Text, Cases and Readings.* 1st ed. New Jersey: Prentice Hall, 1995.

Aust, Anthony. *Handbook of International Law.* Cambridge: Cambridge University Press, 2005.

Boas, Gideon. *Public International Law: Contemporary Principles and Perspectives.* Cheltenham, UK: Edward Elgar Publishing Limited, 2012.

Domingo, Rafael. *The New Global Law.* Cambridge: Cambridge University Press, 2010.

Henderson, Conway W. *Understanding International Law.* 1st ed. West Sussex: John Wiley & Sons, 2010.

Malanczuk, Peter. *Akehurst's Modern Introduction to International Law.* 7th ed. New York: Routledge, 1997.

Nyazee, Imran Ahsan Khan. *Theories of Islamic Law: The Methodology of Ijtihād.* Islamabad: Federal Law House, 2007.

———. *Corporations in Islam.* Islamabad: Federal Law House, 2007.

———. *Islamic Legal Maxims.* Islamabad: Federal Law House, 2013.

Sarakhsī, Shams al-A'immah. *Kitāb al-Mabsūṭ.* Edited by Abū 'Abd Allāh Ismā'īl al Shāfi'ī. 30 vols. Beirut: Dār al-Kutub al-'Ilmiyyah, 2001.

Shaw, Malcolm N. *International Law.* 6th ed. Cambridge: Cambridge University Press, 2008.

Shearer, I. A. *Starke's International Law*. 11th ed. London: Butterworths, 1995.

INDEX

www.ingramcontent.com/pod-product-compliance
Lightning Source LLC
Chambersburg PA
CBHW021005180526
45163CB00005B/1906